Oregon Elder Law

Elder law, estate planning, and probate in plain language

2011 Edition

Published by Salish Ponds Press, LLC
editor@salishpondspress.com
ISBN-978-0-9824564-2-2
ISBN-0-9824564-2-5
www.salishpondspress.com

Oregon Elder Law

Elder law, estate planning, and probate in plain language

2011 Edition

A lightly edited collection of posts from the
Oregon Elder Law Blog

By
Orrin Onken

SALISH PONDS PRESS LLC
FAIRVIEW, OREGON

To Michael Sweeney

Table of Contents

Introduction

I am a probate lawyer who works out of a one-lawyer office in Fairview, Oregon. Fairview is a suburb of Portland. This book is a lightly edited reprint of posts to my blog. The blog is called Oregon Elder Law and can be found at blog.orolaw.com.

I put my blog posts in book form because a lot of elders are not comfortable with computers and the internet.

The book is not intended to be a thorough survey of elder law. I write about what I like to write about. It does, however, provide answers to questions that I hear over and over in my office.

If this book does not answer you questions, you may contact me at

21901 NE Halsey Suite 202
Fariview, Oregon 97202
503-661-2540
oronken@orolaw.com
www.ororlaw.com

—Orrin Onken

Chapter 1: Estate Planning

1. Why it's called an "estate plan."

Couples come to my office and tell me it's time for them to write wills. I correct them and say what they need is an "estate plan." The change of terms is more than just lawyer-talk. People really do need a plan. That's because when you die, property passes to other people in three different ways. A will is one of those ways. A plan takes into account all three.

When you die some property will pass to others because of the way it is owned. A husband and wife usually own their home in a type of joint ownership that allows it to pass automatically to the survivor when the first of the couple dies. I own a house like this with my wife. Let's say I never liked her that much, and I secretly write a will saying that nothing should go to her. When I kick the bucket, she still gets the house because it was jointly owned with a right of survivorship. Husband and wife often have joint bank accounts or joint brokerage accounts that are owned with a right of survivorship. When one of them dies, the other gets the money. In a long term marriage it is common for all of the couple's major assets to be jointly owned with right of survivorship.

Another way that property passes when you die is by contract. I have a contract with Flibinite Life & Casualty which says that if I die in a car wreck Flibinite will pay my wife a hundred grand. The contract is called life insurance, and when I bought it I filled out a beneficiary form naming my wife as the person to receive the death benefit. I also have an IRA retirement plan. The guy who set up that plan and loses my money in the stock market for me had me designate a beneficiary when I set it up. The beneficiary gets the money if I die before I can use it all up. IRA accounts are controlled by beneficiary designation; so are 401(k) retirement accounts. Your bank account may have a "pay on death" feature. This is the same as a beneficiary designation. It is a contractual agreement to give a certain person the money when you are gone.

Beneficiary designations control the money no matter what happens with my marriage. Let's say this time, instead of writing a secret will, I divorce my wife and marry a twenty-two year old roller-derby queen. If I don't change the beneficiary designations before I die, all those companies holding my cash are going to pay—according to contract —the woman I divorced. If the roller derby queen married me for my money, she is going to be royally pissed off at this. That is why I need a plan.

The third way that property passes is by will. Everything that did not go by joint ownership and did not go by contract, goes to the persons named in my will—that is, if there is anything left.

So think about this. Let's say a married couple writes wills that both say, I give everything to my loving spouse, but if he or she does not survive me I give it all to my children: Huey, Dewey and Louie. Then the husband kicks off. (Husbands always kick off first—an average of twelve years before wives.) The house is jointly owned; the bank accounts are all in both names; and the husband's fat retirement plan goes to the wife because she is named as the beneficiary. There is nothing left to go to the people named in the will.

The husband's will is now scrap paper, but think about she wife. She no longer owns the house jointly. The bank accounts are all hers and she has collected the money from the retirement plan. When she dies, everything goes to the people named in her will.

I wrote two wills for this couple. One of the wills was a waste of paper, but the other one controlled everything. The estates of most middle class couples play out just like this. Although the men usually die first, no one can be sure. One of the wills will be important; one of them will not.

2. Who gets my stuff if I don't have a will?

If you die without a will, the state of Oregon has written one for you. A will tells who gets your stuff when you are dead. If you die without a will you are said to have died "intestate." When you die intestate Oregon law determines where your stuff goes. Lawyers have a chart. We find out who survived you, check the chart, and that's where your stuff goes.

By the way, if you die without a will the State of Oregon does not get your property.

If you have a spouse who survives you and the spouse is the parent of all your children, then your spouse gets everything. If you have a spouse who survives you and at least one child who is not the child of your spouse, then your spouse gets half and the rest goes to your children.

If you don't have a surviving spouse your estate goes to your children. If one (or more) of your children died before you did, then the portion that would have gone to the deceased child is split among his or her children. If you never had children, your property goes to your surviving parents. If your parents are gone too, then your brothers and sisters inherit. If your brothers and sisters are dead as well, their children split your property. If you have no brothers, sisters, nieces or nephews, it starts going to your cousins. By this time it is fairly complicated, but your lawyer can look it up.

If someone does not have a relative who can take their property according to the chart, it goes to the State. If there is a relative who is entitled to something according to the chart, but the relative cannot be found, his or her share goes to the Oregon Department of State Lands. Thus, when a relative who would be entitled to property from someone who died intestate cannot be located, the State of Oregon, which is entitled to his or her share, has all the rights that the missing person would have had. That includes the right to be a personal representative of the estate and even to challenge a will.

You can see that if you write a will leaving everything to your spouse, but should he or she not survive you, then to your children in equal shares, and your spouse is the parent of your children, your will states exactly what the law would require anyway. The Oregon law governing intestate distribution is designed to reflect what most people would put in a will if they had gotten around to writing one. That does not mean you should put off doing a will—there are other good reasons for not dying intestate. But you do not have to worry that without a will your family will be denied the benefit of your property. The people you want to get it may not get it, but somebody in your family will.

3. What is Probate and should I fear it?

Probate is the legal procedure for making sure a will is followed, or if there is no will, making sure Oregon law is followed in the distribution of property that belonged to a dead person. Wills give directions to the court about how an estate should be administered and how the property should be distributed, but it is the court that makes it happen. Probate is the broad term for that process.

In probate the property that belonged to the dead person is called the "estate." The dead guy is called "the decedent."

If there is a will, the most important parts when it comes time for probate will be (1) who is named to be the administrator of the will; (2) whether a bond is required; and (3) who gets what. If there is no will, a family member will have to step up to administer the estate, a bond will be required and Orgeon law will determine who gets what property. In most cases, it goes to the decedent's children in equal shares. The people who get the property when there is no will are called "heirs."

Once you have the original will or are sure there is no will, a lawyer writes what is called a "petition" asking that someone be appointed personal representative of the estate and that a bond amount, if necessary, be set. The filing fee for the petition depends upon the value of the estate. The the current filing fee for an estate having between $100,000 and $500,000—a common range for a person who owned a house at death—is is about $500. The cost of the bond also depends upon how much money is in the estate.

If the petition is in order, the court will appoint a personal representative who becomes—for legal purposes—the decedent. The personal representative must then gather together all property that belonged to the decedent, pay all debts owed by the decedent, and thereafter distribute the remaining property to the heirs or the persons named in the will. It is not a fun job, and nobody likes doing it.

Within sixty days of being appointed, the personal representative must provide the court with an inventory of all property in the estate. During the first four months of probate the personal representative must search out and pay the debts that the decedent owed when he died. The four months also allows the personal representative to do those things necessary to distribute the property to the people named in the will. This might mean evicting cousin Mildred, who has been living free in the house for twenty years, and thereafter selling the home so that the proceeds can be divided among the children of the decedent. It might mean selling cars or closing a business.

After the petition is filed, the lawyer sends a copy of it with a special notice to all the people named in the will and all the heirs that would have gotten property had there been no will. This allows heirs to challenge the will on the grounds that the will was executed when grandpa was incompetent or was signed while grandpa had a gun to his head.

At the end of the four months, if no one has challenged the will and all the debts of the decedent have been paid, then it is time to distribute the property to the heirs or the persons named in the will. The lawyer writes another petition asking the court to approve the distribution. If all goes smoothly, the judge approves the distribution, the property is transferred to the people mentioned in the will, and the case is closed.

The personal representative is entitled to be paid from the estate an amount equal to slightly more than two percent of the value of the estate. Attorney fees tend to run between $2,500 and $5,000. That includes writing all the papers for the court, keeping an eye on the debts, making sure the estate property is properly sold, and overseeing the final distribution. If someone contests the will or other problems arise the attorney fees can be much more. The attorney fees, like the fees to the personal representative, are paid from the funds held by the estate.

A lot of people are concerned with avoiding probate. Some want to avoid the expense.

Others want to avoid having their estate documents become a public record. One way to avoid probate is to die without a lot of money. If you die owning very little, there are alternatives to probate that allow the property to be transferred with fewer and simpler court filings. Another way is to own property in a way that does not make it part of your "estate." An "estate plan" may use joint ownership, beneficiary designations, and other legal devices that make probate unnecessary.

A popular way of avoiding probate is by putting your property in a revocable trust. Probate avoidance trusts are too complex to be discussed here, but they do work. The advantage of a trust is that it avoids probate. The disadvantage is that it is more expensive to establish, and it will be administered without the direction of the probate staff in your local county. If you have good and competent relatives who can take care of things without supervision, avoiding the courthouse is a good thing. If your relatives are not so diligent, the lack of supervision is a bad thing. And if your relatives are the litigious types, no legal plan will prevent them from dragging the whole thing into court.

4. What happens to all that stuff in grandma's house?

Grandma is gone. The lawyer is working on how to sell her house and collect the money she had in her retirement account. There are a lot of questions about how to deal with all the stuff in her house but the lawyer doesn't seem to want to answer those questions. Why is that? What is a family supposed to do?

We lawyers call grandma's stuff "personal property." Personal property means her dishes, her furniture, her old car, and that collection of ceramic figurines she was so proud of. Lawyers and judges do not want to deal with grandma's stuff. We want the personal property to go away—quietly with no fighting or bickering.

Despite hating it we do hear about it. We hear about it a lot.

The reason lawyers and judges don't want to hear about personal property is because (1) it is always at the center of family battles, and (2) it is seldom worth any money. Often when a parent dies, the children go temporarily crazy. Sibling rivalries that have lain dormant for years spring up as if everybody is ten years old again. These long-simmering disputes usually make an innocent hunk of personal property the centerpiece.

"I don't care what the will says," one of the children proclaims, "mother always wanted me to have the toilet plunger and after putting up with my brothers and sisters all these years, I deserve it." To the lawyer, these disputes sound crazy. Elder law and probate lawyers charge over two hundred dollars an hour. Simply talking about personal property with a lawyer costs more than the property is worth. The family tells me it is not about the money; it is about fairness. No it isn't. It is about some deep seated family dysfunction that nobody understands except the family members. Lawyers don't get it; judges don't get it. We don't want to talk about it because we have no idea what the clients are talking about and why they care.

Sometimes the family is not fighting but has gone all money-eyed on the theory that mother's collection of Swedish-Korean wind chimes has to be worth at least a hundred thousand dollars. I have overseen the sale of a lot of personal property. I have learned to hate cars, jewelry, and collections. Cars are only valuable if you don't have one and need to go somewhere. If you have to sell grandma's car, hope for low low Blue Book and thank your lucky stars if you can sell it at all. Mother's jewelry may be insured for a bundle, but I can guarantee that nobody wants to buy it. Give it to the daughters and forget it. A collection is the result of having a hobby. The only people who make money off collecting are the people who write those collectors guides—the ones with the ridiculously high values that no one actually pays. Collections are not investments; don't pretend that they are.

When I file a probate petition, I have to file an inventory of the property that belonged to the deceased. The personal representative appointed in the will often looks at me incredulously and says, "But mother's house is packed from floor to ceiling with stuff. How can I inventory all that?" I tell him to walk through the house, wave an arm at all the stuff and say, "personal property, five hundred dollars." I put that in the inventory and no one complains unless it is somebody in the family going wacko over the car, the jewelry, or the figurine collection. Good families get together, split up what they want, and donate the rest. Bad families fight and go to court over it.

Don't get me wrong. I love stuff. I buy nice stuff and don't want to lose it. The fact is, however, that once I have put my grubby hands on the stuff, it is not worth much any more. If I keep it a long time, it is worth even less. Keeping it a very very long time and calling it an heirloom doesn't change that.

So what happens to grandma's stuff? In most cases, whatever the family decides. A judge will decide if you insist, but it will be expensive and the judge will not be happy about being made to do it. You do not want decisions about your grandma's stuff being made by a grumpy judge. Follow your lawyers advice; make the personal property disappear. If family members talk about where it went, nobody else will either.

5. What happens to the property of someone who dies with very little?

After reading my article about probate, a reader asked me what happens when a relative dies with only a bank account, or a car, or some items of personal property. It is a good question.

The amount of complexity required to administer an estate is directly related to the amount of money the dead person had when he or she died. If the person died with nothing, nothing has to be done. The debts of the dead person will remain unpaid forever. The deceased owns no property, so there is nothing to distribute.

If the deceased owns property of certain types, there may be specific legal ways to distribute it.

Bank Accounts

If the deceased had money in the bank, but less than $25,000, a spouse or close relative can fill out a sworn statement requesting the bank deliver the money to the relative. The relative must promise to pay from that money the expenses of the dead person's last illness, expenses of burial, and all debts owed by the person when he or she died. The person who fills out this statement is normally the heir to the estate. Once the heir pays off the funeral expenses, the medical bills, and the dead person's Mastercard bill, the heir gets to keep the rest.

Cars.

If the deceased own cars or trucks at death, those items can be transferred to the heirs by filling out an inheritance affidavit that you can find at the Oregon DMV website. All natural heirs must sign the affidavit.

Accounts with Beneficiary Designations.

Life insurance, deferred compensation accounts, 401(k) accounts, pay on death (POD) accounts, and IRA accounts pass to family members through beneficiary designations. They do not pass through the probate process even if there is a will and a subsequent probate. If there is a beneficiary designation and you are the beneficiary, you get the money.

If the procedures listed do not work because, for instance, the deceased had more than $25,000 in the bank or the deceased left a will which gave the money to someone other than an heir, then there is a short form of probate specifically for the handling of small estates. To qualify as a small estate, the property owned by the deceased on the day of death has to have been worth less than $275,000 with no more than $75,000 in cash or personal property and no more than $200,000 in real estate.

If the estate qualifies as a small estate any person who has a right to some of the estate can file an affidavit of claiming successor. The affidavit is a short form of a probate. It gives the name of the deceased, the names of the heirs, and lists the property and debts of the dead person. If there is a will, the will must be attached. Copies of the affidavit must be sent to the other heirs, the State of Oregon, and all creditors of the deceased. The person filing the affidavit is responsible for (1) sending copies, (2) collecting property owned by the deceased, (3) paying all the debts owed by the deceased, and finally (4) distributing the money to the heirs or the persons named in the will.

The filing fee for a small estate affidavit is currently $78. After accepting the affidavit for filing, the court takes no part in administration of the estate. There is no accounting and no judicial oversight. The administration only comes to the attention of the court if there is a dispute about the handling of the deceased's money. The small estate procedure is a fair amount of work and is easy to screw up if you don't follow the law carefully. It is, however, less expensive and far less burdensome than a full probate. If a person can use the small estate procedure, he or she should.

It is best to consult with a probate attorney about small estates, or to obtain a bank affidavit for the transfer of accounts. The lawyer won't charge that much and it will get done right.

6. Should I put my children on my bank account?

People are all the time telling me, "I put my son's name, on my account so that he can get to my money to pay for my funeral. Most folks create joint accounts or joint owner-ships as a do-it-yourself way to plan for dis-ability or death. However, hearing the phrase "I put somebody's name on . . ." makes Ore-gon elder law lawyers cringe. Let me explain why.

Assume I have a checking account with $50,000 in it, and I decide to put my son's name on it. To me it is a convenience in case I can't pay my bills and he needs to do it for me. To the bank, however, it is a gift of an un-divided interest in the account. As far as the bank is concerned, my son owns that money as much as I do. He can take any amount of money out of the account for any reason he wants, because he owns it too. I may intend that he use the money to pay my funeral ex-penses and doctor bills after I die. He doesn't have to, however, because when I die, he owns it all and can do what he wants with it. I may expect him to divide what isn't needed for bills with my daughter. He might do that, or he might not, and making him do it will require more legal fees than I want to pay.

In addition, once I have put his name on the account, the money becomes a target for people who are trying to get money from my son. If he gets sued, or goes bankrupt, or gets in trouble with the law and has to pay restitution, folks may come around looking for the money in that account to pay his debts.

Now let's say I die. All my money is in the account with my son's name on it. My will says that I want my house sold and the money divided between my son and daughter. Before that happens, though, my bills have to be paid, my funeral has to be covered, and all the expenses of preparing the house for sale have to be paid by somebody. Unfortunately, the money in my account all went to my son because it was jointly owned by the two of us. He doesn't have to pay my bills, pay the expenses related to the property, or split the money with my daughter. He might do that, but he doesn't have to. If he refuses to contribute, he leaves my estate cash poor and unable to pay expenses until the house is sold. This will force a premature sale and a poor selling price.

A parent is often concerned that upon his

or her death, the children will be unable to access accounts quickly enough to pay bills. That is seldom the case. If there is a will, a personal representative can be appointed in plenty of time to take care of expenses. If there is a trust, the successor trustee can take control in a timely manner.

Another concern is having a child able to access funds in case the parent is disabled. This is a serious issue. Conservatorships are cumbersome and expensive. Powers of attorney are unreliable. I have seen joint accounts that have allowed Social Security to be automatically deposited and transferred to care givers years after the elder has lost capacity to handle money. In those cases joint accounts worked beautifully. Beyond that they make me very nervous.

I am comfortable with my elderly clients having a small operating account on which a child is authorized to write checks. The account should normally have under $10,000 and not be the only source of cash for the elder. Other than that, I want to leave the accounts in the name of the elder and use a well-written power of attorney to cover disability issues. If the elder has a lot of money, the protection offered by a conservatorship is worth the expense and paperwork.

Joint accounts should play a very limited role in the estate plan of an unmarried elder. Consider carefully the dangers and weigh them against the advantages. The best way to do this is to make the conversation about joint accounts one you have with your estate planning lawyer, not one you have with your children.

7. Stop writing deeds.

Deeds. They are simple documents that transfer property from one person to another. Anybody can get a deed form, fill it out, and take it down to the county recorder to be recorded. With less paperwork than it takes to get a library card you can transfer the title to a million dollars worth of real estate.

I have a lot of examples of screwed up deeds in my office—so many that I have threatened to open a museum of horrible deeds. To lawyers, they are funny. To the families who have to deal with the consequences, they are disasters.

More often than not these deeds are the result of do-it-yourself estate planning. Somebody decides that instead of going to see a lawyer and paying all those fees, the family should just "put the kids name on" the house. Children use the phrase "put the name on" because they don't want to come out and say the truth: that the children are encouraging the elder to give away the elder's most expensive property while he or she is still alive. Why wait until mom or dad is dead when you can get the stuff right away?

It is not, however, always greedy or ill-informed children who come up with the deed idea. Sometimes it is the elder who has decided he or she needs to avoid probate. This kind of elder has often paid a lawyer for a perfectly good estate plan, and then at the last minute destroys it all with a flurry of amateur deed writing. The children come to me holding mother's will. They are upset because one child now owns everything. I learn that in an effort to avoid probate, mother put that child on the deed to the house. The house was mother's only important asset, so there is nothing left to be distributed to the other children. The gift undid her will.

Think of a will as a coffee canister. On the outside of the canister the owner writes directions about who will get the coffee inside when the owner dies. The owner writes on the can that the coffee will be measured out and divided equally among the owners children. A lot can happen to the coffee before the owner's death. The owner could drink all the coffee so that the canister is empty when he or she dies. The owner could also empty the coffee canister and give all the coffee to her next door neighbor or one of her children. The canister only works to distribute the coffee to the children if there is some coffee in it when she dies. A remarkable number of families get together at the time of mother's last illness and decide to empty the canister. When it doesn't work out because one child ends up with all the coffee and now declares that mom wanted it that way, the other children bring in the empty canister and, pointing to the directions on the outside, complain that they didn't get their fair share of coffee. Sometimes I can help. Many times I cannot.

The most common way to empty the coffee canister is with deeds. Sometimes the elder signing the deed knows that she is giving away everything she owns. Sometimes she thinks that she will continue to own it until she dies and then it will go to the other name on the deed. Sometimes the deed is so incomprehensible and the testimony so conflicting that it is impossible to ascertain what the elder meant.

I want the deed writing to stop. There are ways to make gifts to children while the elder is still alive. There are ways to avoid probate if probate needs to be avoided. Deeds may be part of the plan, but the plan itself needs to be reviewed by a lawyer. Many families have found that the simple deed form from the stationary store that they bought for two dollars, turns out to be—after all my fees are paid to fix the damage—the most expensive money saver in the history of the family.

When it comes time to talk about mother's last illness and what will happen, somebody in the family is going to hint at getting a deed form and putting another name on the house. When you hear that, stop them. Run away. Protest. Don't do it, This is the time to pay for a lawyer.

Chapter 2: Trusts

1. What is a trust?

When discussing legal issues with clients I often get the question, "What about a trust?" Some of these clients want to avoid probate, some want to qualify for Medicaid, some want to protect assets, some want to provide for disabled relatives, and some want to save taxes. Everybody has heard about trusts, but most folks are not sure what they are. Let's talk about the basics.

Most people know about contracts. A contract is a legal transaction between two people. If I want to rent a car, I put up some money, the car rental company puts up a car, and we agree to trade the money for the use of the car. The contract could last for a day or for many years.

A trust is a legal transaction among three people. The first person is the person who creates the trust. This person, called the trustor or settlor, makes the terms of the trust and provides the money necessary to carry out the purposes of the trust. The second person is the trustee. This person takes the money provided by the trustor and agrees to manage and spend it according to the terms and conditions that the trustor wrote down so that the purpose of the trust is accomplished. The third person is the beneficiary. This is the person who receives benefit from the trust. Normally, the trustee has to administer and spend the trust funds for the benefit of the beneficiary.

The basic trust fund baby is created this way. Uncle Scrooge creates a trust for his young nephews, Huey, Dewey and Louie, to help them with their education. Scrooge puts a million dollars in Duckville Savings and Loan and asks the bank's trust department to be the trustee. Thereafter, Duckville Savings, invests the money and spends the income and principal, according to the directions and guidelines contained in the trust, to educate Huey, Dewey and Louie.

Seems simple. Like contracts, the devil is in the details. A full chapter of the Oregon Revised Statutes deals with how to create, administer and terminate trusts. I keep a paper copy of those laws on my desk at all times.

So can trusts do all the things that people think they can? No. Trusts can do some of those things. Trusts can be used to avoid probate, but whether that is a good thing depends on the situation. Trusts can be used to protect assets, but you need to have whole lot of assets that need protection before asset protection trusts become worth the cost and the legal risks. If you have too much income to qualify for Medicaid, an Income Cap Trust will allow you to qualify, but trusts will not permit elders to give away their money and have the government pay for their long term care. Trusts are good ways to provide for disabled relatives and can be used in certain circumstances to give money to a disabled person without disqualifying the person from receiving public benefits. Trusts can save you taxes if you pay a lot in taxes and are willing to give away big chunks of your money to avoid paying taxes on it.

In future writings I hope to address specific kinds of trusts. The important thing to recognize when talking about trusts is that they come in a wide variety of shapes and sizes. You can do a lot of good things with trusts, but like with contracts, if what you hear sounds too good to be true, it probably is.

2. How can a trust avoid probate?

You have heard horrible things about probate. It will be long. It will be expensive. The government will get all your money.

Before you buy into all the hype, review

my article explaining probate in Oregon. You may not want to avoid it at all. For a lot of people probate has advantages, the most important of which is that it forces your family to administer your estate in the way it ought be done. With the help of modern technology, lawyers can get you through probate fairly cheaply, and the time it takes is reasonable for the amount of work that has to be done. Before you run off avoiding probate be sure you know what you are running from.

Let's assume you have read my chapter about probate and no matter what anybody says, you hate the whole idea of it. You can avoid it by being poor. You can avoid it with an estate plan that relies on joint ownership and beneficiary designations. Most people, however, when trying to avoid probate, look to a trust.

If you read the previous article you know a trust is a legal agreement between three people: a person called a settlor who puts up the money, a trustee who takes care of the money, and a beneficiary who gets the stuff that the money buys. So how does this three-way legal relationship let a person avoid probate?

The answer is . . . . drum roll . . . by letting one person serve as three. Instead of three

people, we clever lawyers create a trust controlled by one person wearing three different
hats. You, the settlor—because you settled on
creating a trust rather than going through
probate—transfer all of your property to your
trustee. And who serves as trustee? You do. It
is your job to hold and invest your property
and use it for the benefit of the beneficiary.
And who is the beneficiary? You are, of
course. You give all your property to yourself
to be held for the benefit of yourself for as
long as you shall live. And just in case anything goes wrong, you reserve the right to re-
voke the trust and take back your property
any time you want.

You might well think that this is far too
clever to work in real life. Who would believe
in such a thing? A lot of people agree with
you. The Internal Revenue Service is one of
those people. As far as the IRS is concerned
this is a sham and it will call your trust a "dis-
regarded entity." Money earned by this kind
of trust is taxed as if it came directly to you. If
you owe money, the people you owe can sue
you and get at the money in the trust as if the
trust did not exist. The only people willing to
buy into this scheme are people who live in
the world of probate and estate planning.

Here is how it works. Your trustee—who

is you—owns all your property. Your trust
says that if you die, your trusted son, Harold,
will take over as trustee. It says that when
you can no longer be the beneficiary—you being dead—Harold and his sister, Maude, are
to be the new beneficiaries. The trust tells
Harold to sell all your property, pay your
bills, and divide the money between himself
and Maude. So when you die, the trust lives
on. While you were alive the purpose of the
trust was to keep you happy. Now that you
are gone, the purpose of the trust is to pass
your property on to your children.

Let's compare the workings at death
between a will and a trust using your biggest
asset, your house, as an example.

Let's assume that you wrote a will naming
Harold and Maude to receive your house.
After you die, Harold wants to sell your house
and split the money from the sale with
Maude. He goes down to Infidelity National
Title Company and they explain to him that
the only way he can sign the deed necessary
to sell the house is to be appointed personal
representative of your estate. This means he
has to take the will to the courthouse, pay a
filing fee, and open a probate. He will not be
able to sell the house until he does. After he
starts the probate he will have the court look-

ing over his shoulder from then on to make sure he pays your old bills, files your taxes, and distributes the money exactly as the will says.

Next let's assume that instead of a will you wrote a revocable trust, transferred your house and your other property to the trust, and named Harold to be the trustee when you die. Once again, you are gone, and Harold wants to sell your house and split the money with Maude. He goes down to Infidelity National Title and says my father's trust owns the house and I am now the trustee. The title company will make sure what Harold says is true and then will allow him to sell the house. He can split the money with Maude and the courthouse is out of the loop. You have avoided probate.

That is how it works. You know the downside to probate: higher costs, public filings and the supervision of the court. What are the down sides to a trust?

Trusts cost you more money today. Trusts are harder for your lawyer to write than wills and he has to makes sure that all your property is transferred into the name of the trust. Deeds have to be written and your investment accounts all have to be changed. I explain to clients, "I am going to get your money. You can pay me now by doing a trust or you can do a will and let your children pay me later." Some folks want to make it as cheap as possible for the kids. Others think that because the kids are getting all that money for nothing, the least they can do is pay the costs involved. I don't care. I get paid either way.

One upside to trusts—freedom from court oversight—is a downside if you don't have a trustworthy and diligent person to take over the trust when you die. If the personal representative named in a will isn't doing the job, the court will replace him with someone who will. When you have a trust there is no one to make sure your bills get paid and your property distributed. If Harold, in our example, happens to be living in your house when you die and has no inclination to sell his rent-free home and split the money with his sister, the only way Maude can get her inheritance is to hire a lawyer and sue Harold. In a lot of families, a little court oversight is a good thing.

At the end of the day the choice is yours. Think about what you own, who you can nominate to take charge when you die, and how much you want to pay for estate planning right now. Then collect your questions and talk to a lawyer.

Chapter 3: Powers of Attorney

1. Advantages and Disadvantages of a Financial Power of Attorney

When you sign a financial power of attorney you give a family member or trusted friend the power to make financial decisions and execute documents for you. The surrogate decision maker named in the document can write checks, enter contracts, pay bills and do a wide variety of financial actions on your behalf.

When properly executed in advance of a disability, a financial power of attorney can be extremely useful in protecting an impaired person's money. The power of attorney is also one of the most dangerous and most abused legal tools in the elder care field.

Financial powers of attorney come from various sources. People get them from lawyers, from financial institutions, from office supply stores, and off the Internet. In a power of attorney the signer is known as the "principal." The principal appoints an "agent" to make decisions on the principal's behalf. Most people sign a power of attorney when doing an estate plan as part of planning for incapacity. However, the power of attorney is effective the moment it is signed and remains valid until the principal revokes it or dies. The principal does not have to be incapacitated in order for the agent to use it. The document can be used — or abused — immediately after it is signed.

2. How useful is a power of attorney in real life?

Most people include a power of attorney as part of their estate planning packet. A power of attorney prepares a person for disability by nominating an agent to take care of financial matters if the principal (the person signing the power of attorney) becomes unable to manage his or her own affairs. I have a power of attorney naming my wife as my agent to take care of my finances if I am too ill to take care of them myself. My elderly mother has signed a power of attorney naming me as her agent in case she becomes disabled and can no longer handle her financial affairs. If the power of attorney works as planned, I will step in when my mother can no longer manage her money and I will make the financial decisions she would have made if she had not become disabled. The power of attorney, a relatively inexpensive document, is designed to save a family the stress and cost of going to court to have a formal conservator appointed. But does this work?

I have struggled with explaining how the power of attorney operates in the real world. I used to tell people that it works on a sliding scale. At the low end of the scale, a power of attorney works nearly every time. In the middle it works about half the time, and at the high end it seldom works. Social service agencies are at the low end. If you are the child of a Medicaid applicant with a power of attorney from your parent, the agency will probably give the document only a passing glance before accepting you as the agent. One of the reasons for this liberal attitude is that you are trying to get money for the elder, not from the elder. Society is not going to leave needy elders homeless because of some defect in the language of a power of attorney.

I tell people that banks are somewhere in the middle of the scale. If I walk into a bank holding a power of attorney signed by my mother and want to take money from her accounts, my chances of being successful are about fifty-fifty. Banks are unpredictable. One day I might get the money with no problem. Another day, even at the same branch of the same bank, the manager might tell me they have to send a power of attorney to the legal department for analysis. Power of attorneys that go to bank legal departments often disappear there, never to be seen again.

At the high end of the scale sit brokerages. The chances of me getting into my mother's brokerage account with a power of attorney written by a local lawyer (or worse, a form from Office Depot) are between slim and none. If my mother wanted me to have a power of attorney that would work at her brokerage, she should have signed one of *their* forms, in *their* office, in front of *their* notary. I can't say a brokerage will never honor an outside power of attorney. I will promise, however, that the document will spend a fair amount of time being examined by the brokerage's lawyers before it is honored.

I knew this was how power of attorneys worked, but had a hard time explaining why. Then a Corvallis lawyer named Steven Heinrich put it in a way that I think makes it clear. He once pointed out that a power of attorney is an invitation to agencies, banks, and brokerages to accept the agent as authorized to handle the assets of the principal. Some institutions accept the invitation. Others will not. Government agencies are inclined to accept the invitation; banks accept it now and then; and brokerages most often decline. In the case of my mother and me, neither of us can force her bank or anyone else to accept the power of attorney. She agreed that I can act for her when she signed the document, but that is only half the equation. Only when the bank or other third party agrees to honor her wishes does the power of attorney become truly effective.

So what does this mean to someone planning for disability or worried about the impending disability of a parent. The short answer is that one should not put too much reliance on a power of attorney. It is like a seat belt. It may save your life in certain kinds of crashes, but having it on will not protect you from the consequences of your reckless driving. Planning for disability and death requires a plan, not a document. The power of attorney can be part of a plan, but not a substitute for it.

Chapter 4: Guardianships and Conservatorships

1. What is a conservatorship?

When there is convincing evidence that an impaired elder can no longer manage money, a family member can apply to the court to have a conservator appointed. The court order appointing the conservator will be written to address the specific financial problems facing the elder. In some cases, that will mean that the conservator will completely take control of the elder's money. In other situations, the conservatorship may be more limited, allowing the elder the dignity of controlling some money but restricting the elder's ability to transfer real estate or access investment accounts. After being appointed, the conservator must collect, protect, and spend funds for the elder's benefit.

The person seeking to be appointed conservator must prove to the court that he or she has the skills to manage money. The conservator must also post a bond sufficient to guarantee that the elder's money remains safe. In some cases the requirement of a bond means that even well intentioned and honest family members cannot qualify to be a conservator. In these cases, the court will appoint a professional conservator to do the job.

A court order appointing a conservator denies an elder rights that most of us take for granted. Thus, the elder is entitled to see all the papers filed in court and is given the opportunity to object. Copies of the documents prepared by the lawyer must also be given to the elder's closest relatives so that they too can object. If the elder objects to having a conservator appointed, he or she can hire an attorney, and in some cases the court will appoint an attorney. The elder has the right to make the relative who started the court proceeding prove the case for appointment with clear and convincing evidence.

If the court appoints a conservator, the person appointed must once a year provide the court with a thorough accounting of all money received by the elder and all money spent. Most conservators keep an attorney retained for as long as the conservatorship lasts. If the elder improves so that he or she is once again able to manage money, he or she may ask that the conservatorship terminate. If the elder dies while under a conservatorship, the money in the hands of the conservator is distributed according to the elder's estate plan.

2. What is a guardianship for an adult?

The Oregon courts will appoint a guardian when a cognitively impaired elder is making life-style choices that put him or her in physical danger. Often a guardian is appointed to place an impaired elder in a long term care facility. The appointment of a guardian is an even more severe infringement on personal rights than the appointment of a conservator. A conservator controls only money. A guardian can agree to medical procedures and determine where the elder will live. Thus, the protections for the elder in a guardianship proceeding are even greater than in a conservatorship.

To appoint a guardian, a court must have convincing evidence that the elder's ability to evaluate information is so impaired that the elder cannot manage nutrition, personal hygiene and other basic health care needs. The court must also find that without the appointment of a guardian serious injury or death is likely to result. Thus, the need for a guardian is partially dependent upon the situation in which the elder lives. The court is much more likely to find a threat of serious injury in the case of an elder living alone than in a case of an elder living among family or in a long term care center. As in a proceeding for a conservator, the elder has the right to copies of the documents filed with the court, has a right to object, and the right to an attorney.

When a family member seeks the appointment of a guardian, the court will appoint what is called a "visitor," to talk to the elder, his family and his care givers. The visitor is the eyes and the ears of the court. The visitor will interview the interested parties and report to the judge, giving his or her opinion as to whether a guardianship is warranted and whether the person seeking to be guardian is an appropriate surrogate decision maker. The costs of the visitor are paid by the person filing the guardianship papers.

If no one files an objection and the court visitor reports that the the proposed guardian in an appropriate choice, the court may order a guardianship without a court hearing. If the elder or other family members object, there may have to be a hearing in which evidence is presented by both sides. If a guardian is appointed, the guardian will be required to report once a year to the court on the condition of the elder.

3. How disabled does a person have to be before a guardian will be appointed?

When the law appoints a guardian for an adult it takes away the most important and intimate rights we have come to expect as citizens. Only being sent to prison is worse. A guardian can tell you where you have to live, tell you when you have to go to the doctor, and tell you what medical treatments you must endure. Because of the intrusiveness of having a guardian appointed, the law provides many protections to make sure that guardianships are not ordered unless they are absolutely necessary. You might think that one of those protections would be a clear and unambiguous legal standard for appointing a guardian. If you thought that, you were wrong.

In order to have a guardian appointed for an impaired elder a court must find that the elder is "incapacitated." Incapacity is defined in Oregon Statutes. In order for you to understand the problems that lawyers have in guardianship cases you should read the definition.

> "Incapacitated" means a condition in which a person's ability to receive and evaluate information effectively or

to communicate decisions is impaired to such an extent that the person presently lacks the capacity to meet the essential requirements for the person's physical health or safety. "Meeting the essential requirements for physical health and safety" means those actions necessary to provide the health care, food, shelter, clothing, personal hygiene and other care without which serious physical injury or illness is likely to occur.

We learn one thing from the definition. We learn that the only impairments that will support a guardianship are those related to either thinking or communicating. You can be paralyzed from the neck down, but a guardian won't be appointed if you can still make decisions and communicate your wishes.

Dementia arrives in stages. How cognitively impaired do you have to be before the law steps in? The second part of the definition suggests that the impairment must be so severe that physical injury or illness is likely to result. This leads to the common scene in which a relative has applied to have a guardian appointed for a resident who is in a long term care facility and who is not refusing medical treatment. If I represent the elder I ask the director of the care center whether the elder in his care is currently in danger of physical injury. To say that the elder is in danger condemns the care center; to say that the elder is safe says that a guardian is unnecessary.

It is fairly clear in real life that the degree of impairment necessary for a guardianship is related to the conditions in which the elder lives. An elder who insists on living alone in a remote cabin will have to show greater cognitive skills than one who lives in a full-service long term care facility.

When the Oregon Statutes don't answer the question, lawyers turn to reported cases from the Oregon Court of Appeals. The Oregon case interpreting the definition of incapacity is called *Shaefer v. Shaefer*. In *Shaefer*, the elder was an eighty-six year old woman who lived alone with a large number of cats and a dog. She had some memory loss plus confusion, her house smelled of pet urine, and she was not taking her prescribed medicine. The court held that Mrs. Schaefer did not need guardian.

The court said that for a guardian to be appointed for Mrs. Schaefer the judge would need clear evidence of three things:

 1. That the elder has severely impaired perception or communication skills.

 2. That the elder cannot take care of basic needs to an extent that it threatens life or health,

 3. And, that the cognitive impairment is the *cause* of the life-threatening disability.

Mrs. Schaefer had some cognitive loss and she was refusing medical treatment, but she was not refusing treatment *because* of the cognitive decline. She was refusing because she did not like the side effects of the medicine. The smell of cat urine in her house was the price she paid for the companionship of her cats, it was not the result of dementia.

The Oregon probate judges read the *Schaefer* case with great interest, and then ignored it. I have not seen or heard about *Schaefer* having much of an impact. I think that the best approach to the real standard for a guardianship comes from Tim McNeil, a lawyer and popular presenter in the Oregon elder law field. He points out that guardianships and conservatorships are called *protective proceedings* because the point is to protect vulnerable elders. Judges will follow the law, but they are not going to let fear of being overturned on appeal prevent them from stepping in when they see an elder truly in danger.

No one wants a guardian and elders usually object when served with the papers that start a guardianship proceeding. I think, at the end of the day, the guardianship cases succeed or fail on whether the elder is in immediate danger. If you claim a guardian should be appointed and can show a clear threat to the health of the elder that can be eliminated by appointment of a guardian, you will probably prevail. If the threat is speculative, or looms only in the future, you may not.

4. When to file a Guardianship or Conservatorship.

I have clients show up at my office saying that employees at the care center or service providers are saying that their elder family member needs a conservator or guardian. They come to me to start that process. My response is to ask what task are they trying to accomplish that cannot be done without the court order appointing a guardian. Who is standing in your way and saying you can't do what you want to do without court authority?

The fact is that a lot of elder care is done with a wink and a nod. People who are disabled with dementia enter contracts for long term care and live for long periods of time in care centers. Children take over the finances for their disabled parents using joint accounts or a power of attorney. Problems do occur—such as when the children clean out mom's account to buy drugs—but most of parent-child financial arrangements work out just fine.

(Elder financial abuse is real. Those who commit it need to be chased down and walloped many times with ax handles, but most children do not steal from their parents.)

I don't advise asking a court to appoint a guardian or conservator until there is no choice. If you get the call from Tuality Hospital telling you that grandma is being held in the geriatric psych unit and that they will not release her unless there is a court appointed guardian to make placement decisions, then your have to get yourself to the courthouse. If mother is sending all her money to internet scammers in Nigeria and the bank tells you that she is over twenty-one and can do whatever she wants, then it is time to go to the courthouse.

On the other hand, if your mother has dementia but is willing to go to a care center, you should talk to the people at the care center. Even if mother is not technically competent to understand all the fine print on the long term care contract, chances are she will be admitted anyway. Don't go to court unless there is no other choice.

If you talk to the people who work for the probate courts, you are likely to hear that the judges and others who work there are the last bastion of protection for the disabled and elderly. There is some truth to that, and in the bad cases the court plays a crucial role in protecting the vulnerable. On the other hand, the courts provide neither care nor money for care. The courts provide oversight, but at an enormous cost. Filing fees are significant, and attorney fees make any trip to the courthouse an expensive proposition. The paperwork required to satisfy court oversight goes on and on. There exists a small cadre of attorneys, visitors, professional fiduciaries, and experts who make a living off the state court system for protecting the vulnerable. I am one of those. You do not want your mother's money going to keep all these people in business unless you have no choice.

There is an axiom in my business that the court will not allow prophylactic protection in fiduciary proceedings. That is a fancy way of saying that the court will not appoint a guardian or conservator because the elder might need one in the future. The need must be immediate and serious. This should be your standard as well.

This is not to say that you shouldn't go see an Oregon elder law lawyer until you have hit the brick wall. A consultation with a lawyer early in the process can set you in the right direction and educate you about your real-life options. An elder law lawyer not only knows the law of guardianships and conservatorships, he or she knows local court procedures, how things work in practice (rather than in theory), and the attitude toward various kinds of cases taken by the local probate court. Sometimes, knowing the personalities of the people who will be handling your legal paperwork is as important as knowing the law. It is well worth the money to get this kind of insider insight from a lawyer early in the process.

To sum it up, go to a lawyer at the first sign of trouble and go to court when you have no other choice.

5. What is a bond and why do I have to post one?

In the world of Oregon elder law, a bond is required in almost all conservatorships and many estates. When you are appointed a conservator, you are put in charge of funds belonging to an elder who can no longer handle money. The bond is a promise by a bonding company to the court and the impaired elder to replace any money you steal. So if the first thing you do as conservator is take the money and fly to Paraguay, the bonding company is on the hook for the loss. In an estate you are appointed personal representative—sometimes called executor—to manage the money that belonged to the dead person for the benefit of the heirs. If you steal the money instead, the bonding company pays off.

Because of the cost, most wills ask the court to dispense with a bond and courts normally grant the request. If, however, the person who died did not waive bond, or left no will at all, you will have to post a bond to guarantee that you don't run off with the money.

People have the mistaken idea that getting a bond is related to the applicant's honesty. That isn't the case. Bonding companies offer bonds using the same standards used by credit card companies in offering credit. The availability of a bond is dependent upon the wealth and credit history of the applicant. When someone comes to me wanting to be appointed conservator in order to protect grandma's million dollars, the very first thing I do is call my bonding company. My client could be as upstanding and honest as the day is long, but if she is a store clerk who lives in an apartment, there is no bonding company in the world who is going to bond her for a million dollars. She simply does not have enough money and credit worthiness to get the bond. In an estate, the same thing applies. Grandpa's will may name cousin Bob to be the personal representative, but if Bob can't qualify for the bond someone else will end up doing the job.

In some cases none of the people interested in the impaired elder or the estate can qualify for the bond. In those cases, the lawyer handling the conservatorship or the estate has to look for a professional to do the job. I am not convinced that professionals do a better job at being a conservator or a personal representative than family members, but professionals all have established relationships with the bonding companies. If they don't, they are out of business.

Even when a family member does qualify for a bond, it is expensive. Depending upon the credit worthiness of the applicant, the bond for a middle class conservatorship or estate can be a couple thousand dollars a year. Consequently, lawyers are always looking for ways to reduce the amount—and therefore the cost—of the bond. The most common way of doing this is by restricting assets.

Let's say grandma dies owning a $350,00 home and a $50,000 investment account. Little Huey qualifies for a bond, but wants to reduce expenses so there is more money to distribute to him and his brothers. Huey will ask the court to restrict sale of the real property so that it cannot be sold without court order. That will protect the real estate. He will then ask that the bond be set at $50,000, enough to cover the investment account. The savings to the estate will be significant. Huey could also put the cash in a restricted account. This would also reduce bond costs.

Huey has to be careful though. Filing those motions to restrict sales of real estate and restrict accounts increases attorney fees. He needs to make sure the savings are not eaten up in additional lawyers fees. The key will be in not spending more money trying to reduce the cost of the bond than the bond would have cost in the first place.

Bonds are important protections in estates and conservatorships, but they also prevent some good and honest family members from serving. When a family member can serve, he or she must examine carefully both the cost of the bond and the cost of the legal strategies to reduce it.

6. What is a court visitor?

In guardianship cases, Oregon law requires that a "court visitor" interview the elder, the caregivers, and the family. The visitor —the independent eyes and ears of the judge —then makes a report to the court. Often the court visitor is the most important witness in the case. The lawyer with a court visitor's report on his side is likely to win, and the lawyer going against the recommendation of the court visitor is left scrambling for a paid expert willing to testify that the court visitor is wrong.

The process for hiring the court visitor varies widely from county to county. In Multnomah County there are two court visitors. You pay their fee when you file the guardianship petition, and the probate department decides which visitor gets the case. The current fee is about $425. In other counties the lawyer must select a visitor from a list and pay the visitor directly. In the larger counties the court visitors are psychologists or social workers. In counties where money is short, the visitor may be a local volunteer with time on his hands, or a judge's secretary.

If no one objects to a guardianship petition and the court visitor recommends it, the court will order a guardian appointed without ever hearing from the disabled elder. If, however, the elder objects to the guardianship or wants an attorney, the visitor will communicate that to the court. The court will then advise the lawyers and set the matter for a hearing. It the elder cannot afford an attorney, the court will assign one from a list of volunteers.

At a hearing on a guardianship, the report of the visitor comes into evidence and the visitor testifies as an expert. This means that the visitor can stay in the courtroom, watch the other witnesses, and comment upon what they say. The position of visitor is so powerful in some counties, that lawyers write their guardianship petitions with the visitor in mind.

Judges like having the visitor present as an unbiased witness. Putting the visitor's testimony at the center of guardianship proceedings, however, has two problems. First, visitors err of the side of protecting the elder. A guardianship is their hammer, and soon every social problem involving elders begins to look like a nail. Secondly, visitors seldom spend significant time with the elder. Because of the unique position of the visitor, it often takes the testimony of several professionals and family caregivers—people who may have spent months or years with the elder—to overcome the testimony of a visitor who saw the elder for less than an hour.

The use of the visitor streamlines the guardianship process for the lawyer and the litigants, but the efficiency is not without costs. Any person contemplating a guardianship for an adult should talk frankly with his or her lawyer about how the visitor system works in the local court and what approach should be taken if the visitor does not support the guardianship.

Chapter 5: Oregon Elder Law Lawyers

1. Who are the Oregon Elder Law Lawyers?

It has come to that. Your elderly parent is giving all her money away to a televangelist, leaving the stove burners on for days at a time, or wandering in the street in her nightgown. You have tried to talk to her. She refuses to change her behaviors and adamantly refuses to enter a care center. You have talked to your brothers and sisters and to her bank. Everyone agrees that someone has to be appointed by the courts to protect her from herself. You need a guardianship or a conservatorship.

You are entering a world in which several professions and several arms of government uneasily interact. You may think it is simply a matter of hiring a lawyer and letting the lawyer take care of things. Guardianships and conservatorships are seldom that easy. This chapter is intended to educate you about the lawyers who work in this field

Elder law lawyers come from a variety of places. There are elder law firms, sole practitioners, lawyers from full-service firms who practice elder law, lawyers who do elder law and other things, and lawyers who will do anything that comes in the door. It is worthwhile to take a look at each type.

Elder Law Firms

In Oregon, Multnomah County is the only county that has firms of lawyers that do only elder law. Because the demand for elder law is not great, elder law firms are small compared to firms in other areas of law. Multnomah County has three of them: Fitzwater & Meyer, Nay & Friedenberg, and Davis, Pagnano. Fitzater & Meyer is the largest of them, and as of this writing, the firm web page lists ten lawyers.

The elder law firms offer the full gamut of elder law and estate planning services. They employ paralegals and generally use technology to provide quality service at a fairly reasonable price. The lawyers at these firms tend to charge an hourly rate higher than the sole practitioners, but when the cases are over their bills are not necessarily higher. Some clients like the security the firms offer, while other prefer the intimacy of working with a sole practitioner.

Sole Practitioners

I am one of these. I practice out of a small office in Fairview, Oregon with the help of a legal assistant. There are a quite a few sole practitioners doing elder law. Many of them limit their practice to a certain aspect of elder law. One local attorney takes only contested guardianships and conservatorships. Another refuses to do contested cases, handing only cases that do not require hearings. Sole practitioners tend to charge a lower hourly rate than firm lawyers, but they sometimes lack the technological tools and support staff that streamline legal services. I like to think that my bills come out lower than those from the firms, but there are other sole practitioners in which that is clearly not the case.

Lawyers from full service firms that do elder law

Some large full-service firms, the kind that represent businesses and professional sports figures, have a lawyer or two on hand to handle elder law issues. These lawyers tend to concentrate on probate and the conflicts that arise when rich clients die and pass on their money. Those cases are close enough to elder law to enable the full-service firm lawyer to tackle an elder law case now and then. The big firm lawyers are always intelligent and well trained. Sometimes, however, they lack intimate knowledge of the court staff and procedures. This means they spend more time on simple things and charge a very high hourly rate for doing so.

Lawyers who do elder law and other things.

Some communities simply cannot support a lawyer who wants to do elder law full time. Thus, if a lawyer wants to make a living, he or she does other kinds of law as well. Some excellent elder law lawyers in small towns also do divorce law. Sometimes a lawyer is transitioning from one kind of practice to another and during the transition period does both. The lawyers I have seen who fall into these categories tend to do a fine job at a reasonable price.

Lawyers who do anything that comes in the door.

Some lawyers offer to do whatever you need done. They will get you out of jail, get you divorced, get a personal injury settlement after your slip-and-fall at the grocery store, and establish a conservatorship for your demented parent. The smaller your community, the more likely it is that you will find lawyers like this. If this is the only kind of lawyer available to you, then you have no choice. If you live in a more urban area, find someone who practices elder law on a regular basis.

Conclusion

People generally overestimate the impact their choice of lawyer will have on a case. The law is the law. The facts of your case are what they are and you are not supposed to make up new facts in order to win. The lawyers job is to know what the law is and present the facts to the court in the most positive light. It ain't rocket science.

If you need an elder law lawyer, first find a lawyer who actually practices elder law. Your business lawyer or that great guy who helped you beat the drunk driving charge may not be the right person to help you with a guardianship or conservatorship. Next, pick a lawyer you like. There are a lot of us out there. You should not have to put up with someone you do not get along with. And finally, choose someone you can afford. When you and your lawyer are both comfortable with how the fees are going to be paid, the relationship has a lot better chance of going well. It is very often true that as the relationship goes, so goes the case.

2. How to choose an elder law lawyer.

Some people are lucky enough to have a friend or co-worker who has had a positive experience and can recommend an attorney in the elder law field. Often, however, that is not the case, and the family faces the daunting task of scouring the Yellow Pages and the internet for an appropriate person.

We all know that the Yellow Pages contain advertising. Lawyers buy ads and hope the amount of business the ads bring in will be worth the monthly cost. Virtually all third party websites that provide information about elder law lawyers are the same. Lawyers pay to have their names listed. If you go to the AARP web site looking for an attorney you will find a list of attorney's who have paid to be on the list. In the case of the AARP, it costs a lot. The same applies to ElderLaw Answers, Oregon Elder Law Attorneys, NOLO Press, and many many more. If there is a list of lawyers on the web, odds are that the lawyers paid to get on it.

Most of the web sites listing lawyers shy

away from rating them. That is not the case with Avvo. Avvo lists all lawyers. It lets us claim our listing and fill in the blanks about our experience and specialties. It also gives lawyers a ranking based upon some mathematical formula. Due to my colorful history with the Oregon State Bar—a history that can easily be found by running my name through Google—I am ranked at the bottom with the warning "extreme caution." Who knows, Avvo may be right—after all they have math on their side. On the same page as my abysmal ranking is an ad for another lawyer in my neighborhood. He gets his picture on my page because he paid for an upgrade. At the end of the day, it is still about advertising.

You might look for a lawyer who belongs to the appropriate organizations. Many elder law lawyers belong to the National Academy of Elder Law Attorneys. I belong to NAELA. I read the newsletters and the journals they send me. I wouldn't have to do those things to belong. I could just send in the money once a year and the organization would be quite happy take it and list me as a member. I belong to the Guardian/Conservator Association of Oregon, the Oregon Gerontological Association, the Oregon Mediation Association, and the Elder Law Section of the Oregon State Bar. Does belonging to these organizations make me a better elder law lawyer? Probably. But not that much better. What counts is what we do at work, not what we do in our spare time.

Here is my theory. Find some elder law lawyers in your neighborhood and look at their web pages. Get a feel for them. Some folks like a firm—it gives them a sense of security to see several lawyers and a lot of staff. Other people are more at home with a sole practitioner or a couple of partners. These clients like the intimacy of the small practice. Then meet with the lawyer and see if you like him or her. There are a million lawyers; there is no excuse for having one you don't like. Talk about your problem and see if you are comfortable with both the legal plan the lawyer devises and the cost. If it doesn't feel right, get out and try somebody else.

If you follow my plan, chances are you will be okay. Most lawyers are going to look at your case and come up with the same answer. People win cases because they have good cases, not because they have good lawyers. You don't want a lawyer who can't find the court house, but in the elder law world, you don't need Clarence Darrow either.

3. How to scare away an elder law lawyer.

Lawyers want and need clients. Our professional magazines are filled with ideas about how to get them and how to keep them. Clients pay our bills and keep us in business. However, we want good clients with good cases. Very few of us are so desperate that we have to take anybody who comes through the door. I have been astounded for years how difficult some people make it for me to want to take their cases. Many people who want a lawyer and need a lawyer are going without because they are doing a horrible job during their first contact with the lawyer.

A remarkable number of people who contact me give me some version of the following tale:

"I don't have any money to pay for a lawyer but this case is easy and you should be able to get the other side to pay your fees. The last lawyer I had was incompetent so recently I have been representing myself, but the judge is crooked and keeps ruling against me. Oh, and did I mention, I need to be in court tomorrow afternoon."

When I hear this sort of thing—and trust me, I really do hear it—I run for the hills. I would rather give up the profession than represent this person.

I have developed five rules to follow when you first approach a lawyer about taking your case. Following them won't guarantee the lawyer will take the case, but ignoring them will guarantee that he or she won't.

Rule One: Don't lead with the fact that you can't pay.

Lawyers are suckers for a good story and can often figure out a way to get paid if you can't pay them. But you have to sell them on the case first. When you start out with how broke you are, the lawyer's interest starts to drop immediately. You do have to be honest about your ability to pay; you don't have to make it the first thing out of your mouth.

Rule Two: Don't evaluate your own case.

People are always telling me how easy it will be for me to win their cases. They scare me when they do that. I practice law for a living and I know how easy it is to lose a case. I don't want to hear from an amateur what a slam dunk it is. Studies show that people in a dispute uniformly overvalue their own position and undervalue the position taken by the other side. Clients do this and lawyers do this. When you first talk to a lawyer about your dispute show him that you know there are two sides to the dispute, that your view is not the only view possible, and that you are willing to work with the lawyer to set realistic and achievable legal goals.

Rule Three: Don't bad-mouth other lawyers.

I had someone explain to me the other day that he had to fire his previous lawyer because she was grossly incompetent. I asked who that was, and the potential client named one of the best lawyers in the elder law field. His harsh criticism of his previous lawyer made me wonder what he would be saying about me three months from now. I wasn't willing to risk it and sent the potential client down the road. Being critical of others seldom makes you happy and almost never helps you accomplish goals you would like to accomplish. I say this after having tried it over and over, waiting for good results to happen. They never did. If you walk into my office bad-mouthing other lawyers, the judges, and the other parties in the case all you do is convince me that you like to bad-mouth people and that once you leave my office you will probably be doing it to me.

Rule Four: Go see the lawyer before you have lost the case.

People have a constitutional right to represent themselves. I support that right and wish the best to anyone who wants to do it. But if you do it, follow through to the end. I am plagued with people bringing me a stack of unorganized paper and a story about how they wrote a whole bunch of letters to the judge and now there is a ruling against them. I look at the case register and see that they did a horrible job—failed to pay fees, misunderstood the rules, and missed important deadlines. They represented themselves, they lost, and now they want me to go in and un-lose the case. It can't be done.

Rule Five: Don't wait until the last minute.

I refuse to work for clients who tell me over the phone or in the initial meeting that

"there is a court hearing tomorrow afternoon." Legal proceedings provide ample notice of hearings. I have a calendar and I
schedule my time. It takes me a long time to
create a file and prepare for a hearing. I won't
tell all my other clients that their work should
wait because this new guy couldn't get around
to coming in until the day before a hearing. I
turn down good cases from paying clients because they waited until the last minute. Other
lawyers do it to.

Some clients make me feel like they respect my time, they are interested in my
opinion of the case, and they want me to be
properly paid for my work. I love working for
those clients. If you want to hire a lawyer, try
being one of those clients. Lawyers will be
falling all over themselves wanting to work
for you.

4. How elder law lawyers get paid.

Lawyer's fees depend upon what you want
done and who you want to do it. Some lawyers charge more than others. Higher priced
lawyers justify the higher charges on the theory that they are better lawyers. Like all the-
ories, some people buy it and some don't. In
this post I explain the four basic methods of

paying lawyers, the role of court costs in the price of litigation, and the way lawyers pass on their business overhead to you.

Lawyers fees come in four basic types: flat fee, hourly, phase fees and contingency. A flat fee is a set fee for a certain service. An hourly fee is exactly what it sounds like—you pay for the time the lawyer works on the case, usually by six minute intervals. Phase fees are variations on the flat fee with a set amount payable for each "phase" of a proceeding. Contingency fees are fees based upon a percentage of the money the lawyer recovers in the case.

Flat Fee

A flat fee is straightforward. I might offer to do a middle class estate plan including wills, powers of attorney, and advanced directives for $700. That is a flat fee. I collect half at the beginning of the job and the other half when the client is satisfied enough with my work to come in and sign the documents. In the old days flat fees were the norm for almost all legal work. Then certain high powered clients got the feeling that lawyers were getting a lot of money and not working very hard. They said, "wait a minute," we want to pay by the hour and thereby make sure that our lawyer is actually working on

our cases. A few decades later most lawyers
were working by the hour. Now the tide is
changing again, as more and more Bar asso-
ciations advise lawyers to abandon the hourly
rate. The attractive thing about a flat fee is
the certainty. You know what your legal services will cost and you aren't scared to call
your lawyer for fear of the next monthly bill.
The drawback is that a highly automated lawyer with good support staff may be able to do
your $3,000 flat fee legal job and get to the
golf course faster than you can get home from
the appointment.

Hourly Fee

The hourly fee pays the lawyer for the
time he or she puts into the case. Time is kept
in tenths of an hour and billed monthly.
Hourly rates for elder law in Multnomah
County run between $200 and $250 per
hours, although I have heard rates as high as
$350 per hour. The advantage of the hourly
rate is that you only pay for the time the lawyer works on your case. The disadvantage is
that you pay for every minute the lawyer
works on your case. Whether this works out
for you will depend upon to what extent the
lawyer has billed earlier clients for the job of

learning the issues that arise in your case. If your case is simple and all the issues are familiar to your lawyer, the hourly billing system works to your advantage. If unusual issues arise and your lawyer has to do legal research or make unexpected trips to court, the hourly rate works against you. In the latter case, you end up paying for the lawyer's education so that he can do his or her work more efficiently for the next client. This is great for the next client but not so great for you. The disturbing thing for most clients faced with hourly fees is the uncertainty. It looks like a carte blanc for the lawyer to pick up your file and do a little work on if for $230 an hour any time the office bank account is a little low.

Phase Billing

Phase billing is a type of flat fee billing designed to fit cases in which the amount of work involved is unpredictable. Most cases that will be filed in court fit this description. When someone files a probate for a deceased family member or a for an elder with dementia, the lawyer and client do not know whether other interested people will object to the proceeding or whether court appearances will be necessary. Thus, the lawyer and client agree that the client will pay a flat fee for each "phase" of a proceeding. The lawyer might charge $1,200 for filing of a probate, serving all the people required to be served with the petition, obtaining the tax identification number for the estate, publishing notice in the newspaper, and supervising the initial inventory. If there is a missing heir, the client will be charged an additional fee for an heir search. If there is a creditor who claims to be owed money and the claim is disputed the attorney would receive a flat fee for that process. Phase billing fee agreements tend to be complicated because the agreement must carefully set out the lawyer's and the client's responsibility during each phase of the case. On the other hand phase billing allows the client to know both the best case scenario and worst case scenario. The advantage for the lawyer is that it allows the lawyer to use office efficiencies and relieves him or her of the drudgery of time keeping. I hate time keeping and am working on some phase billing for my practice. Phase billing is not widespread in Oregon elder law at this time, but it is coming.

Contingency Fee

When a lawyer signs up to do work on a contingency, he or she takes as a fee a percentage of any recovery from the other side. For contingency to work there has to be an other side and the other side must be capable of paying. Contingency fees are common in the world of personal injury where insurance makes defendants able to pay awards. Contingency is less common in the Oregon elder law world. Some lawyers will do a financial elder abuse case on a contingency if it is a strong case and the alleged abuser has a lot of money. Some lawyers will take a will contest —a case in which a will is challenged as being obtained by fraud or undue influence—on a contingency. This is about it for contingency in the elder law and probate world.

Costs and Expenses.

In addition to lawyers fees you must be aware of costs and expenses. The client is responsible for court filing fees, publication fees, fees for personal service on certain parties, other court costs, and the costs of experts, if necessary. Costs can be significant, and you should discuss them with the lawyer at the outset.

Lawyer's Overhead

In addition to lawyers fees, some lawyers charge the time for legal assistants, copying and postage. These kind of charges vary a lot from lawyer to lawyer and you should discuss them ahead of time. I have a large corporate client that strictly prohibits these kind of charges on the theory that they are attempts to transfer normal overhead to the client. I think the theory is a good one, although it severely limits my ability to pay my assistant twenty dollars and hour and bill her services at a hundred, thereby pulling down a nice eighty bucks an hour for doing nothing. If your lawyer is at the top range of hourly rates and is also charging you for a lot of overhead, you might want to wander down the road and talk to someone else. There are lots of lawyers out there; you can find one that will treat you fairly.

Conclusion

The key to a good relationship with your lawyer is to talk openly about the fees and any concerns you have. You don't want to be in the dark about what your lawyer is going to cost you and no lawyer wants to do work while worrying that he or she will not get paid. When both sides are at ease about the fee issues, both the case and the relationship go a lot better.

5. *How many lawyers does it take to establish a guardianship or conservatorship.*

By now you know where elder law lawyers come from and how they get paid. I will now assume that have hired an elder law lawyer to help you get a guardian appointed for your elderly demented parent who is no longer safe living alone. Your lawyer learned all about your parent and filed a petition in court asking that you be appointed to make decisions for your parent. You intend to move your parent to a long term care center. Before you know it there are lawyers everywhere. Let's take a look at where they all come from.

Your Lawyer

You know where your lawyer came from. You learned about the various kinds of elder law lawyers. You avoided any of the behaviors described in my earlier article about how to scare away an Oregon elder law lawyer. Then you found a lawyer you liked and hired her.

A Lawyer for the Disabled Elder

After your lawyer filed the papers neces-sary to begin the guardianship, he had the pa-pers personally served upon your disabled parent and mailed to the other members of the family. The papers served upon your par-ent gave directions on how to object to the proceeding. One of the papers is a blue form which stands out from the others. It is the form your parent uses to object to having a guardian or a conservator appointed.

Sometimes the elder signs the blue objec-tion form. Sometimes a concerned relative signs the form and claims the elder did it. Elders served with a petition for the appoint-ment of a guardian have been known to emerge from deep comas long enough to sign the blue objection form. Lets assume that your elderly parent received the form, de-cided you were just out to get her money, and vows that she will never leave her home.

Your disabled parent might go out and hire an elder law attorney using the same method you used to find your attorney. Your parent's lawyer would then defend the elder's right to make decisions for herself. If your parent objects by filling out the blue form, but does not hire a lawyer, the court may appoint one for her. The court uses a list. The lawyers on the list have agreed to take court appointments with the understanding that sometimes the lawyer will get paid and sometimes the lawyer won't. I am on the list. Being on the list is a risk, but we do it because we think that the elder in these cases should have a lawyer on her side.

Now we have two lawyers. Your lawyer filed the case. Your parent objected and the court has appointed a lawyer from the list to represent your parent. But we aren't done yet.

The Lawyer for the Professional Fiduciary

Soon after your parent gets a lawyer, your lawyer calls you into his office and gives you fourteen reasons why you should not be the guardian for your parent. The most convincing reason is that being a guardian for your objecting parent may well destroy the parent-child relationship. Your lawyer suggest that you ask a professional guardian to step in. There is a small industry consisting of social workers, nurses, and psychologists who make a living being guardians and conservators for the elderly. Your lawyer recommends one and you agree.

Soon you find that the professional guardian suggested by your lawyer has her own lawyer. The professional's lawyer comes from one of the local elder law firms or is a well-established sole practitioner who does nothing but elder law. Elder law lawyers regularly recommend certain professional guardians and conservators to their clients, and professional guardians reciprocate by hiring those elder law lawyers to represent them in other cases. If your lawyer said that Fred Feelgood would probably be a good professional for your parent, it is probable that Fred has hired your lawyer to represent him in other cases.

Now you have a lawyer, your parent has a lawyer, and the professional fiduciary has a lawyer. How many lawyers does it take to keep your elderly parent safe? The answer is three. If your parent has money, all of them will expect to be paid from your parent's cash. And there could be more.

Lawyers for the other relatives and government agencies.

When your lawyer filed the papers to have a guardian appointed, he gave copies of the papers to several of the the elder's relatives, the state of Oregon, and sometimes the U.S. Department of Veteran's affairs. Any concerned relative or disgruntled government agency is entitled to file papers in the case and have their issues heard. Thus, that angry brother of yours who thinks your parent should never be allowed to eat salt gets his day in court. If your elder is receiving government benefits, the agency in charge may have something to say. The courtroom is quickly filling with lawyers.

Conclusion

The old Chinese blessing wishes you a life without lawyers. Before you go off to file the papers to start a guardianship or conservatorship, be aware that you are putting the wheels of justice in motion. We lawyers are like owls —we see motion and swoop in to feed. What started as a simple visit to one Oregon elder law lawyer can end with a courtroom full of them. This is not to suggest that you shouldn't do it. If an elder is in danger, you may have no choice. But be warned, you may end up in a courtroom full of lawyers, every one of them wanting to be paid from the funds of the disabled elder. The point is that filing for a guardianship or conservatorship attracts expensive professionals. Don't do it unless the result you want to achieve is worth the risk that you are taking.

Chapter 6: The Other Participants in Elder Law Cases

1. The Judge and the Court Staff

I have written about the kinds of lawyers who practice elder law. I have written about the number of lawyers who might become involved in an Oregon guardianship or conservatorship. It is time to talk about the the various non-lawyers who might show up in your case.

Judges

In Oregon, guardianships and conservatorships are handled in the probate department of the circuit court. In the larger counties there is one judge assigned to head the probate department. That judge may do all probate matters, or administer the probate department with the help of other judges.

The judges preside over hearings in contested cases. They make rulings on motions and sign the orders that establish a guardianship or conservatorship. It is the judge's job to make sure the law is followed, and that every person gets a full and fair chance to be heard. There is one local Oregon judge who is fond of stating that she is the last line of protection for the aged and the disabled.

Oregon judges do a good job. Because probate judges specialize in probate cases, they know the law well and, as far as I can tell, administer justice as well as fallible humans can do. Nobody is perfect and no judge I know claims to be an exception. My experience is, however, that Oregon judges are intelligent, hard working, always prepared, respectful of the litigants, and fair.

Court Staff

If one were to look through probate files at an Oregon courthouse, you might see hundreds of approvals, orders, and other documents which appear to have been examined and approved by a judge, but in fact were not. The courts see the same kind of documents so many times, that the probate staff is often charged with examining the documents, determining their compliance with law, and either approving them directly or recommending that a judge approve them. A probate staff member may either have a stamp with the judge's signature and be authorized to use it, or may bring the matter to the judge with a recommendation—at which point the judge signs off on the matter without really looking at it.

Judges work hard to treat lawyers and litigants with equal respect and courtesy. The probate staff is more willing to play favorites. Lawyers who hang around the probate court a lot and get friendly with the staff have an easier time getting documents signed than those who don't. Lawyers who have dealt honestly and straightforwardly with the court for years will have their requests granted with barely a glance, while those who have been disingenuous with the court, or rude to the court staff, will have a hard time of it.

(If you are considering hiring an Oregon elder law lawyer, ask the potential lawyer the name of the probate coordinator in the county where you are going to file. If he or she doesn't know, move on to somebody who does.)

I had an assistant once who asked me, "is probate law the same in every state?" I answered that probate law has been pretty much the same since Roman days, but we don't get paid the big bucks because we know probate law. We get the big bucks because we know the probate coordinators in all the surrounding counties. People are local. So is justice.

There is no trick to dealing with judges
and the probate staff. Be honest and forth-
coming with the judge. Be courteous and
helpful to the court staff. If you can do both
those things there should be nothing you
need worry about in dealing with a court.

2. *Professional Guardians and*
Conservators.

There is a Bill Cosby skit in which Bill ob-
serves that parents faced with bickering children to not want justice—they want quiet.
Judges often have a similar attitude when it
comes to families battling over who should be
appointed guardian or conservator for an
aging family member. The judge doesn't want
to hear about all the dirty laundry and figures
that if the family cannot agree, everybody will
be better off with a neutral party. That neutral party is almost always a professional. Elder law lawyers refer to guardians and conservators as "fiduciaries." Some fiduciaries are
family members. The ones I am talking about
today are professional fiduciaries. They do it
for a living and they charge for their services.

Where do Professional Fiduciaries Come From?

Professional fiduciaries are people who have set up small businesses serving as guardians, conservators, and trustees in cases where there is no family member available to play that role. They tend to be trained in medicine or the social services, but there are no requirements for being a professional fiduciary other than the ability to get a bond and the ability to get appointed. Several prominent fiduciaries in Oregon used to work as nurses. Others hold masters degrees in social work. Some simply learned the profession on the job by working for other professional fiduciaries.

Although there is no license required to become a professional fiduciary, most of the professionals in Oregon belong to the Guardian/Conservator Association of Oregon. The web site contains a list of its members. If you go to the list you will see that I am a member. I am not a guardian or a conservator, but I deal enough with the professionals that I want to keep up with what they are doing.

In a guardianship or conservatorship the professional fiduciary needs his or her own lawyer. Professional fiduciaries build relationships law firms and use the same ones over and over. The fiduciaries give work to the law firms, and the firms give work back to the fiduciaries. If you are an elder law lawyer it is good for business to have a fiduciary or two who likes to hire you. If you are a fiduciary, it is good for business to have a lawyer or two who will call you when a case needs the skills of a professional. One hand washes the other.

One interesting aspect of the connection between law firms and fiduciaries is that a professional fiduciary can file a petition for the appointment of a guardian or conservator even if no one in the family wants it to happen. For example, a fiduciary with connections in the medical community might get called when a medical provider is suspicious about the welfare of an elder. The fiduciary goes to her favorite law firm and causes a guardianship petition to be filed. A few days later the family is inundated with legal papers from a person completely outside the family who is asking to be appointed guardian for the disabled elder and expecting to be paid, along with the attorney, from the funds of the elder. There have been some complaints about this process, but the courts have tended to allow it on the grounds that it does result in protection for elders.

The professionals, like law firms, have their own personalities. Some are sweet social worker types who try to make everybody happy. Others are tough—stepping in to make the difficult decisions when the people in the family cannot. Almost all fiduciaries do business as sole proprietors or small partnerships. Some run their businesses out of their homes.

Fiduciaries, in addition to having connections with law firms, also develop connections with arms of government. Some fiduciaries will work only within the state court system. Others work primarily with the U.S. Department of Veterans Affairs and its system for providing benefits for disabled vets. Tension between the state and federal government in this area, translates into tension among the fiduciaries attached to each. An elder law lawyer thrust into one of these disputes among agencies and their favored fiduciaries spends as much time on the politics of the case as she does on the law.

What do the Professionals Do and What Does it Cost?

Professional guardians make medical and placement decisions for disabled elders. Professional conservators collect, secure, and manage the money for elders who cannot do that themselves. They charge between sixty-five and an hundred dollars an hour. They often employ bookkeepers and caseworkers who charge less than that. They do whatever is required by the court order appointing them and report yearly to the court. Once appointed, they are extremely difficult to get rid of.

Conclusion

In the right circumstances, having a professional fiduciary take care of your love one can be a blessing. You go back to being a child or a grandchild or a friend and the professional makes the hard decisions. In the wrong case it can be a nightmare. For a period of time, I made a good living litigating against professional fiduciaries who had clear and firm ideas about what should happen to an elder and were not about to let meddling loved ones or even the law get in their way. If you must invite a professional fiduciary in your life, try to get Anne Sullivan and not Nurse Ratched. In the beginning it can be hard to tell the difference. Demand references and talk to people in the field to make sure the person will work for your family.

3. United States Department of Veterans Affairs

I wrote earlier about state court judges and the court staff. I now want to write about a government agency that is completely and utterly indifferent to anything that happens in state court. It is the U.S. Department of Veterans Affairs.

The U.S. Department of Veterans affairs—the USDVA—is a federal agency that provides medical care and a lot of other benefits for veterans. Some veterans receive disability payments due to service-related disabilities and are incapable of handling the money on their own. For these veterans the USDVA has a payee system under which it nominates a family member or a professional fiduciary to hold and administer the disability money for the veteran.

Some times the professional fiduciary selected by the USDVA will not need all of the veteran's disability money for his needs and the funds will start to accumulate in the account controlled by the fiduciary. The USDVA might then ask the fiduciary go to state court to establish a conservatorship. In other cases, family members go to state court asking for a guardianship or a conservatorship because the veteran has other funds that need to be protected, and they want the USDVA disability benefits controlled by the same conservator. In both of these situations the Oregon State court system and the USDVA collide. The results are seldom pretty.

In an earlier article I mentioned the state court judge who considers her court the last line of protection for elders and the disabled. Well the USDVA has a different view about how much protection state courts offer. To the USDVA the state court system is one in which overpaid professional fiduciaries and lawyers empty the coffers of the disabled without providing much of anything in return. People closely aligned with the state courts don't think much of the USDVA system either. Fiduciaries used to working in the state court system think the USDVA fiduciaries are under-trained, inexperienced, and overworked. Professional fiduciaries who are well respected in the state court system may be despised by the USDVA, and fiduciaries who are believed to walk on water by the USDVA may be looked upon as common criminals in the state court system. The key for you is to recognize the dispute without getting involved in it.

The important thing to remember is that the USDVA is allowed under federal law to ignore anything and everything that state courts do. You cannot subpoena USDVA records or personnel. State court orders can be completely ignored by the USDVA and routinely are. Therefore, if the bulk of the money going to a disabled person is USDVA money, you cannot go to state court to get control of it.

Let me say this again in capitals. YOU CANNOT USE THE STATE COURTS TO GET CONTROL OF USDVA MONEY.

I repeatedly see family members and their lawyers going into state court saying that they want honest old Uncle Henry to be conservator for disabled cousin Darrell so that Henry can control and administer the money coming every month from the USDVA. It ain't going to happen. The USDVA will decide who is in charge of that money, including accumulations of it in bank accounts, and there is nothing your local judge can do about it.

Not only will the USDVA not allow state courts to interfere with the administration of veteran's disability payments, it seldom allows its employees to appear in state court proceedings at all. Thus, if your proof that grandpa has Alzheimer's depends upon testimony from his medical providers at the US-

DVA hospital, you may lose your case. The only way I have gotten USDVA providers into court has been by begging and pleading with the USDVA lawyers, and when they finally agreed, the witnesses were accompanied by a USDVA lawyer to make sure he or she didn't say anything that wasn't in the agreement I made with them. That was a couple years ago, and rumor has it that since then the USDVA has become even more reticent about allowing its employees into state court.

So here are the guidelines
- Don't get involved in the friction that exists between the state court system and the USDVA
- If there is a conflict between a state court and the USDVA, the feds win—every time.
- Don't expect to ever win a case in state court using evidence provided by the USDVA.
- Money that comes from the USDVA stays in its control forever and there is nothing you can do about it.

After I explain all this to clients they say, "I hate the person appointed by the USDVA to handle my father's disability money. What can I do?" The answer is political. Complain a lot and write your congressman. As an Oregon elder law lawyer who hangs around state courts, there is nothing I can do for you.

4. Social Security

Social Security provides retirement income for nearly all Americans over the age of sixty-five and provides disability income for millions of disabled people no matter what their age. Thus, Social Security provides at least some income to most elders or disabled persons who become subject to a guardianship or conservatorship.

When an elder or disabled person cannot manage his or her money, Social Security uses a "representative payee" system that allows a responsible relative or a professional to receive and spend Social Security income for the disabled person. A relative applies to Social Security to be appointed "rep payee" for a disabled person, and if the facts support the need for a fiduciary, Social Security will send the money to the representative. The paperwork is minimal and the annual accounting requirements are fairly simple.

While the U.S Department of Veterans Affairs does not play well with the state court system, the Social Security Administration does. If a state court appoints a conservator to handle the money of a disabled person, Social Security will generally honor the state court decision and, upon application, make the conservator the representative payee of social security benefits. The U. S. Department of Veteran's Affairs, as I noted earlier, is seldom so cooperative.

You need to keep these relationships in mind when you are determining what kind of fiduciary your disabled elder needs. We know that a guardian makes medical and placement decisions, while a conservator takes control of money. If the elder's money all comes from the federal sources—Social Security or veterans disability—there is probably no need for a conservatorship. The existing federal systems already provide the mechanisms to protect the money. If you establish a conservatorship to handle non-federal assets, Social Security will honor the conservatorship by naming the conservator as rep payee for Social Security income. This puts all the money in one set of hands. The Veterans Administration, on the other hand, will probably not cooperate in this way and may ignore the state court proceeding.

The rule is that you do not need a conservatorship if the only income of the disabled person is federal money—whether that be Social Security, veteran's disability, or both. If the elder has assets other than from federal money—let's say a big investment account and some real estate—then a conservatorship may be necessary to manage those assets. Once the conservatorship is established the conservator can take charge of the Social Security money, but he will not get control of veterans benefits (without making his or her case directly to the U.S. Department of Veteran's Affairs).

Conservatorships are expensive and messy. Before you wander down that path be sure what assets you want to conserve and whether the protection offered by a conservatorship is worth the cost of the legal proceedings. When making the calculation, don't include federal money—Social Security and veteran's benefits—because that income is conserved through the federal system. Once you have removed the federal component take a look at the costs of the state court proceeding. If the cost of the conservatorship exceeds ten percent of the the amount of money to be protected, look for another way.

5. The Oregon Department of Veterans Affairs, the Public Guardian, and Seniors and People With Disabilities

I have written about lawyers, professional fiduciaries, the courts, the U.S. Department of Veterans Affair, and Social Security. In this section I want to talk about three agencies. I combine the three because in practice the agencies to not show up often in guardianship and conservatorship proceedings, but when they do they play and important role.

The Oregon Department of Veterans Affairs.

The Oregon Department of Veterans Affairs (ODVA) is a state agency that provides a low cost alternative to a professional fiduciary for Oregon veterans. Under the right circumstances the ODVA will serve as a conservator for Oregon veterans. The ODVA is not associated with the U.S. Department of Veteran's Affairs, but the ODVA and the USDVA tend to get along fairly well. Because of this amicable relationship the USDVA is often willing to appoint the ODVA as representative payee for federal veterans disability payments. If a disabled veteran has money being paid to him by the USDVA and also has income subject to state court supervision, one way to put all the assets into the hands of the same fiduciary may be to ask the ODVA to handle both sets of funds.

The ODVA takes cases based upon its funding and criteria set within the agency. It won't take every case it is offered. However, if your disabled elder is receiving disability income from the USDVA, you should always check to see whether the ODVA would be a good choice as a fiduciary. The services provided by the ODVA are as good as any private fiduciary in the state and cost far less. If your disabled Oregon veteran is not receiving federal benefits, but there is no appropriate family member or the case presents particular problems, the ODVA may still be the solution you need.

Being a state agency, the ODVA is subject to the budget fluctuations of state government. It's ability to take on further cases at any one time may depend on politics and the current budget.

The Public Guardian

Multnomah County has a public guardian. The public guardian serves as a fiduciary for a certain number of the elderly and disabled when there is little money and no appropriate family member. The ODVA serves veterans. The public guardian serves those who are profoundly mentally incapacitated, unable to care for themselves, and currently at high risk due to abuse, exploitation or extreme self-neglect. The public guardian has its own criteria for which cases it will accept, and like the ODVA is subject to budget constraints.

Seniors and People With Disabilities (SPD)

Seniors and People with Disabilities (SPD) is an arm of the Oregon Department of Human Services. SPD takes reports of elder abuse or of elders in dangerous living conditions. It investigates abuse and neglect. It reports severe cases of elder abuse to law enforcement for prosecution. Prosecuting criminals, however, only benefits disabled elders in the deterrence effect prosecution has on other would-be criminals. SPD does not normally initiate guardianship or conservatorship proceedings, does not obtain restraining orders to stop further elder abuse, and does not pursue civil remedies against those who have taken advantage of the disabled or elderly. Recent changes in the law have made it easier for DHS to instigate guardianships or conservatorships, but it is still rare for the agency to do so.

Most care and protection of the elderly is done in the private and charitable sector of our communities. Churches provide far more support for and monitoring of the elderly than does government. Most long term care centers are privately run. The elder law bar is made up of private practice attorneys. SPD does not work effectively with any of these private sector communities.

Although SPD is a player in the elder law world, it is seldom effective except in the most severe cases. Next time you suspect elder abuse, spend an hour or so trying to find the correct number and then call it in. You will see what I mean. In the average guardianship or conservatorship, SPD is nowhere to be seen.

Chapter 7: Mediation of Probate Disputes

1. Mandatory Mediation in Multnomah County

Alternative Dispute Resolution—mediation and arbitration—has been used by the courts in Oregon to help resolve civil cases for a long time. If you sued somebody, you didn't get at trial before a judge or jury unless you first went through arbitration or mediation. That was true everywhere except in the probate courts. As of February 2010 in Multnomah County that changes.

The new local court rules now provide that the judge or any attorney in the case may put a contested matter into mediation. The new rules set out the procedure for mediation and who may serve as a mediator.

While lawyers outside of the probate world are comfortable in mediation, we who practice in Oregon elder law have not embraced mediation eagerly. I have attempted to talk other lawyers in disputed elder law cases to hire an elder law mediator but have had minimal success. One of the problems I faced in convincing other lawyers to embrace mediation is that court time in probate is not that hard to get. The probate world has no jury trials. Most issues can be heard and decided in a few hours. Mediation, on the other hand, can be a lengthy process. It often entails more than one meeting, any one of which can last several hours. Mediation, I believe, leads to better results; it does not however, in probate, necessarily lead to cheaper results.

I have known for some time that mediation was coming. In preparation, I took a course in mediation put on by the Multnomah County Court system and then a longer mediation course taught by Stan Sitnik at Portland State University Department of Conflict Resolution.

Stan's course completely changed my views on several subjects. Two of them are important.

First, I misunderstood mediation. I thought of mediation as being something like a judicial settlement conference where the mediator would listen to both sides, offer suggestions for settlement, and opine on the value of each side's argument from the vantage point of someone who had been doing probate law since Cain killed Abel. This kind of "evaluative" mediation does exist, but it is not exactly in the forefront of current practice. Mediation being currently practiced is a process whereby the mediator steers the parties toward effectively negotiating a resolution themselves. The parties—not the wise mediator—create the solution.

In my class, one young woman opined that she did not think she could be a mediator, because in the role playing she could clearly see how the parties should resolve their differences. She was unable to keep quiet about her solution while the parties struggled to arrive at an obviously inferior answer. Stan suggested she get over it.

Second, before attending Stan's course I thought I was a reasonably competent negotiator when it came to settling cases. In fact, I sucked. My idea of negotiation was to try to get the other side to take a position. I would take a position somewhere away from that, and we would grimly compromise toward a middle. It is a lousy technique that lacks intelligence, stifles creativity, and makes people mad at each other. I am still fairly embarrassed that for so long I went to work every day to deal with conflict resolution and had so little understanding of how to effectively negotiate. Mediation helps people become effective negotiators for their own interests.

I am currently a quiet member of the Oregon Mediation Association. One section of the association deals with elder mediation. I suspect that as mediation begins to play a greater role in probate litigation, elder law mediators will see a lot more work. How this will work out for litigants remains to be seen.

2. *Probate Mediation: An Update*

I am now an approved Probate Mediator for Multnomah County probate disputes. In the fall of 2010 I got practical experience in the Multnomah Small Claims Mediation program where experienced mediators held my hand and did what they could to impart to me the lessons they had learned over the years. The process has opened my eyes to new ways to looking at dispute resolution.

I often refer to my probate practice as family law at the other end of life. In traditional family law parents fight over the custody of the kids. In my probate practice the kids fight over the custody of their parents. Emotions run high in my cases. Sometimes the cases are driven by a real legal dispute. In others, however, the law is clear, and the case is driven by sibling rivalries and family resentments that have festered for years. Litigation offers a solution—albeit one imposed on the family by a person in black robes. Mediation offers healing.

I recently spent a morning in a mediation in which six siblings faced the problem of how to care for an aging father. They brought with them decades of hurt feelings, suspicion, and festering resentments. I watched as a skilled mediator helped the group find a solution that worked for all of them and actually brought them together. It was not what a court would have ordered. It was a solution designed by the people who would have to live with it. My bet is that it will work better than any solution a court would have or could have fashioned.

Some lawyers are embracing mediation. Some are looking for any way possible to avoid it. The bulk of them, however, are supportive but confused. The procedures are new and kinks have to be worked out. We know that disputes in guardianships, conservatorships, and probates must go to mediation before they will be heard by the court. The confusion centers around when mediation notices must go out, what the notices must contain, how to choose the mediator, and how to schedule the mediation. These are not insurmountable issues but we lawyers—having gone to so much college to get to where we are—dislike learning new stuff. We will get over it and in five years mediation will be as accepted in probate as it now is in family law.

So here is mediation in a nutshell. If your lawyer files a paper that creates a dispute—usually an objection to something another lawyer filed—then the dispute must go to mediation. The party who created the dispute must provide the other side with the names of acceptable mediators. The other side can object to mediation, accept one of the proposed mediators, or propose its own list of acceptable mediators. If the parties cannot agree on a mediator, the court will appoint one. The parties can pick any person they want (with some exceptions), but the court must pick from the list of court-approved mediators. I am on that list.

Once a mediator is selected the parties must mediate for at least three hours. If an agreement is reached the mediator will write it up. The parties then have seven days to repudiate the agreement. If no one repudiates, the agreement, it is rewritten as a judgment by the lawyers and presented to the court. If the parties do not reach agreement, or if one of them repudiates the agreement, the case goes to court.

My opinion is that if your lawyer says you

have been ordered to mediation, celebrate. You have a chance to do something good. Good things do come from the court; just not as often.

Chapter 8: Long Term Care

1. The Suffering of the Dutiful Daughter

Nursing homes, adult foster homes, and assisted living arrangements are the public face of long term care for the elderly. In the real world, however, most long term care is performed by families. When there are siblings charged with taking care of a parent the duty usually falls upon the eldest daughter. This is statistically true across cultures and across generations. It is true even when a younger daughter or a son might be the more qualified care giver, a fact that often leads to strife among the siblings. In my own family, I have seen a younger daughter chafe under the injustice of seeing her parent and the other children all looking to the older sister for leadership regarding care issues, ignoring the superior capabilities of the younger. It isn't fair, and it isn't likely to change.

More often than not it is the oldest daughter who comes to me to say that the family can no longer handle the pressures of providing long term care. The crisis is often the result of increasing levels of dementia in the elder—loss of cognitive ability that makes the elder increasingly incapable of cooperating in her own care. In these cases the daughter faces asking the court to appoint her conservator to take control of the parent's money and use it for the costs of professional long term care. When I explain the process for becoming a conservator, I must also explain the curse of the dutiful daughter.

It is not unusual, I explain, that the one person willing to stand up and protect the elder ends up hated by everybody. A court proceeding is public, intrusive, and embarrassing for the elder. The dutiful daughter——the only member of the family willing to step up and do the right thing—ends up hated by the parent because he or she cannot see through the fog of dementia that the proceeding is meant to help. Other family members turn on the dutiful daughter as they see the parent's money being locked away to be used only for the long term care needs of the elder. Family members who have been using that money as if it were their own will not be above holding a grudge against the person responsible for bringing the gravy train to a stop.

Relatives, whether or not they be dutiful oldest daughters, seldom refuse to proceed with court action out of fear of the curse, but it is important that they be steeled for it before we sign the papers.

2. What is Medicaid and Will it Pay for Grandma's Nursing Home?

Some questions are awfully big. This is one of them. I can only skim the surface of the complex rules and benefits that fall under Medicaid, but I will give it a try.

Medicaid is federal money administered by the states to provide a variety of social services for the poor. For the elder law lawyer, most questions about Medicaid relate to whether an elder qualifies to have the government pay for long term care in a nursing home or similar facility. Medicaid is not Medicare. Medicare is health insurance that everybody gets when they turn sixty-five. Bill Gates gets it.

Medicaid is for the poor. At this writing, to qualify for Medicaid an elder must be sufficiently handicapped to need care in a facility, have less than $2,022 of monthly income, and have less than $2,000 in available assets. The figures in Medicaid calculations change frequently.

Medicaid planning is a strategic effort to make a person poor enough to qualify for

Medicaid and thereby have the government pick up the cost of long term care. This normally involves spending enough of the elder's money to get assets below $2,000, yet preserve the elder's standard of living as much as possible. The strategic spending of money to obtain Medicaid is called "spend down."

When calculating the value of assets owned by an elder, certain assets are not considered. These are exemptions. Depending upon circumstances, a house may be exempt, or a car. Money in the bank—over the $2,000 limit—is never exempt. Thus, one way to do Medicaid planning would be to use money in the bank to buy, pay-off, or improve an exempt asset. Sometimes assets can be turned into income.

Families often come to elder law lawyers with this request: mother wants to give her house and all her money to her kids ("she always wanted them to have it") and then have the government pay for her nursing care ("after all she paid taxes all these years"). There are smart lawyers out there working for the state of Oregon whose job it is to make sure this doesn't happen. Here is the basic rule: YOU CANNOT GIVE AWAY YOUR MONEY AND THEN ASK THE GOVERNMENT TO SUPPORT YOU.

The exception to the basic rule is that you may be able to do it if you have quite a bit of money and a brave elder law lawyer. If the government doesn't challenge the strategy you win. If the government challenges the strategy and you win, the lawyer gets a good chunk of your cash for fighting the good fight. If the government challenges the strategy and you lose, the lawyer still gets paid and you don't get Medicaid.

The application of the basic rule can cause a lot of tension in families. Grandma is often an easy touch, willing to buy new cars for her unemployed kids and bail the drug-addicted grandchildren out of jail. It can come as a shock to the family, that Grandma has to quit handing out cash and use her money for her own care needs.

The answer to the question posed in the title to this entry is yes. Medicaid will pay for grandma's long term care. The first catch is that Medicaid will only pay if grandma cannot pay from her own money. The second catch is that grandma cannot make herself unable to pay for care by handing out cash to her relatives. Beyond that it gets pretty complicated.

I tell my elders when they come in and I see that they are not millionaires, "From now on you can give birthday and Christmas gifts worth up to $100 per person. Beyond that your ability to give away money is over. Write a will. Bake a cake, but don't give away money." Not only is this a good Medicaid strategy, it also lets them know which of the relatives are coming over because they really want to visit.

Chapter 9: Elder Abuse

1. Elder Abuse Restraining Orders

Oregon Law provides that a disabled person or a person over sixty-five years of age who has been a victim of physical or financial abuse can ask the court for a restraining order that prevents the abuser from continuing to abuse the elder. There is no filing fee, and the clerk of court is required to provide the necessary forms. The request must be heard by a judge within one day and the restraining order can be based solely upon the testimony of the abused elder or the elder's guardian. It is a powerful weapon.

As with anything in the law, the devil is in the details. So what does the elder have to tell the judge to get the restraining order? The elder must show that he or she has been the subject of abuse within the previous 180 days. Abuse is one or more of the following:

- Physical abuse resulting in injury;
- Neglect that leads to physical harm;
- Abandonment by a care giver or other person with an obligation to care for the elder;
- Willful inflicting of physical pain;

- Using derogatory names, profanity, ridicule or coercion;
- Wrongfully taking or wrongfully threatening to take away money or property;
- Non-consensual sexual contact.

After showing that the elder has been subject to abuse in one or more of the forms described above, the elder will then have to convince the judge that he or she is in danger of future abuse by the same person. If the judge finds that abuse has occurred and there is a danger of further abuse the court must act. The judge will issue a restraining order preventing the abuser from abusing, intimidating, or interfering with the elder. If necessary to prevent further abuse, the court can prohibit the abuser from entering any premises where the elder might be found. If the elder lives with her abuser and owns or rents the home, the abuser my be ordered out of the home with a policeman sent to help with the removal.

When the abuser is served with the restraining order the sheriff will also give him or her a form to fill out to object to the restraining order. Most people accused of elder abuse will object. The person accused of abuse has thirty days in which to file the objection. Once the objection is filed, a trial will be held within twenty-one days. Although the judge has a duty to protect the elder from a traumatic confrontation with the abuser, the trial takes place according to the same rules that govern other trials. Both sides call witnesses, offer exhibits, and argue their side of the case. After hearing all the evidence from both sides the judge will uphold the restraining order, dismiss it, or change it to reflect the evidence. The judge may also require one party to pay the attorney fees incurred by the other.

If the abuser, before or after trial, violates the provisions of a restraining order he or she will be arrested and charged with contempt of court. At the very least, the abuser will get a free ride to jail. What happens after that will depend on the severity of the violation.

Because elder abuse restraining orders are so powerful and so inexpensive, creative elders and their lawyers have pushed the limit of the law. I have seen a local judge refuse to grant an elder abuse restraining order because a neighbor of the elder used profanity in an argument about a property line. The observation was the law was not intended to protect anyone over sixty-five from rude neighbors. On the other hand, a judge in Multnomah County recently issued a restraining order preventing protesters in front of a business from shouting at the elderly owner. My feeling is that most judges will be ready and willing to protect an elder from real threats, but unwilling to apply the law to every angry interchange in which one of the participants happens to be over sixty five. A lot of sixty-five year olds are in pretty good shape and can take care of themselves—and the judges know it.

2 Financial Elder Abuse and the Obligation to Say No

Hitting up one's relatives for money is a time honored survival skill in every culture. Most people give up the practice when they reach middle age, but all of us have certain family members who simply can't wean themselves from the parental checking account. In the past we just felt sorry for these family members and let them go about their business. In today's world, with severe legal penalties for elder financial abuse, the ancient practice of finagling money out of elderly relatives can put a person on the wrong end of a very ugly lawsuit. Here is how it works.

Elder financial abuse means wrongfully taking money or property from a person who is disabled or over sixty-five years old. That covers a lot of people. We can't retire at sixty-five any more, but we are nevertheless protected by Oregon's elder financial abuse law.

To be elder financial abuse the taking must be "wrongful." So what makes it wrongful? Stealing is wrongful. Embezzlement, extortion, and armed robbery are wrongful. Withholding money that belongs to the elder is wrongful. But those kinds of wrongful taking are not so common, and when they occur we normally call the police. Where the lawyers come swooping in is when money is taken from an elder using what the law calls "undue influence."

"Undue influence" is a complicated concept that has been imported into the law of elder financial abuse from the world of will contests. In Oregon, a will can be set aside if it was the result of undue influence. Since the passage of Oregon's elder financial abuse law, courts have decided that undue influence is also a good concept for deciding whether taking money from and elder was wrongful. Those court decisions have broadened the protection of elders, made it dangerous to accept gifts from elderly relatives, and given new legal weapons to children dissatisfied with their parent's estate plan.

You take money by use of "undue influence" if you have a "confidential relationship" with an elder and thereafter use that relationship to get money transferred to yourself. A confidential relationship is a slippery legal concept. You might have a confidential relationship because the elder wants you to be on his or her bank account, wants you to be an agent on a power or attorney, or simply takes your advice on financial matters. If you have a confidential relationship with an elder and the elder wants to give you money or property (without having received independent and professional legal or financial advice) you may have a legal obligation to say no. If you fail to say no, you can get sued for three times the amount you received and be required to pay the attorney fees incurred in suing you. If you are close to an elder relative and have some influence over his or her financial decisions, taking gifts of money from that person can be risky.

How do you protect yourself? Easy, don't accept gifts from elderly relatives or other disabled people unless the gift is wrapped in Christmas wrap and fits beneath a tree. If the gift doesn't fit that description send the elder to an Oregon elder law lawyer who has never been your lawyer. Then let the lawyer do the work. If you elderly mother thinks you should be on the deed to her house, or really wants you to have a new Mercedes, send her to a lawyer. Failure to do so could end up with you being sued.

You think, "But why would a loving parent who gave a lot of money to their kid, then sue to get it back?" The answer is that the parent doesn't sue. Somebody does it in his or her place. To see how that happens and why lawyers love to do it, keep on reading.

3. Elder Financial Abuse: Who is doing the suing?

Above I explained elder financial abuse and your obligation, at some point, to say no to the elder who wants to give you money and property. After the explanation you asked, "But why would an elder who loved me enough to give me money then turn around and sue me for financial elder abuse?"

The answer is that the parent doesn't sue. The parent becomes disabled with dementia and the parent's conservator or trustee sues. The conservator might sue because the gifts have made the elder unable to pay for long term care or unable to qualify for Medicaid. The conservator might also sue to get the money back so it can go to the elder's heirs when he or she dies. Lets say a grandchild talks demented grandma into giving her a whole bunch of money. The children of grandma get a conservator appointed to handle grandma's financial affairs. The conservator then sues the grandchild to get the money back so that it can go to the children according to the will when she dies.

After an elder has died, the representative of the estate may sue those people who received money from the elder while she was still alive. In these cases, the object is to squeeze money from one heir and give it to another. The child who received money is forced to give up her inheritance to get rid of the elder financial abuse case. Disgruntled heirs like this idea and lawyers can make a lot of money doing it.

Let's say your elderly mom gets most of her legal advice from her hairdresser. Let's say further that you are on her bank account so you can help with her bills and she has named you her power of attorney. She comes home from the beauty parlor one day and tells you she will lose all her property to taxes and probate unless she puts your name on the deed to her house right away. She says she wants you to have her house when she dies, tells you to get a deed written, and says not to tell your brothers about it. Ignoring my earlier advice about accepting gifts from elders, you do what she says.

Mom then dies without a will. The money in the checking goes to you because your name is on the account. The house goes to you because your name is on the deed. And your brothers are furious.

The brothers could challenge the deed to you claiming that you had a confidential relationship with your mother and "unduly influenced" her to give the house to you. This case would be somewhat like challenging a will. A lawyer might, however, try a different strategy. He gets one of your brothers appointed personal representative of your mother's estate and then sues you for elder financial abuse. By claiming elder financial abuse the brother can seek triple damages and attorney fees. In addition, he has the inflammatory claim that you abused your mother. Rather than looking like greedy heirs, the brothers look like knights on white horses coming to the rescue of your poor abused mother.

Cases like the one described above come in all sizes and shapes, but they share one characteristic. In each of them the elder financial abuse claim serves the interest of heirs (or those who take pursuant to a will or trust) who are dissatisfied with their share of the elder's estate. What once would have arisen in a will contest or a suit to set aside a deed is brought to court as elder financial abuse.

There are elder abuse cases in which someone is truly trying to get back from bad people money that those people took from a helpless elder. These cases are not as common as you think because those kinds of bad people are criminals who have spent all the money on drugs and couldn't pay it back if they wanted to. Many elder abuse cases are will contests in disguise, serving the interests of people trying to maximize their inheritance.

About the Author

Orrin Onken is a probate lawyer who practices in Fairview, Oregon. More articles about elder law can be found at his blog – blog.orolaw.com.

Made in the USA
Charleston, SC
24 March 2011